The Christmas Story

Drawn directly from the Bible

Edward A. Engelbrecht
Gail E. Pawlitz
Editors

CONCORDIA PUBLISHING HOUSE • SAINT LOUIS

Copyright © 2011 Concordia Publishing House
3558 S. Jefferson Ave., St. Louis, MO 63118-3968
1-800-325-3040 www.cph.org

Edited by Edward A. Engelbrecht and Gail E. Pawlitz

Illustrations by Corbert Gauthier, Cheri Bladholm, and Phil Howe
© Concordia Publishing House.

"Oh, Come, All You Children" Setting: Melvin Rotermund. Copyright
© 1984 Concordia Publishing House.

Printed in Heshan, China/047365/300311

1 2 3 4 5 6 7 8 9 10   18 17 16 15 14 13 12 11

The Christmas Story

For many years God promised a Savior. He gave this promise through many prophets. Then the time came for God to fulfill His promise. It was just the right time.

This is Joseph and Mary. They know the Savior is coming. They know He will be great. But they do not know how He will come, how He will appear. Do you know how the Savior will appear? That's the next part of the story. I wonder . . . what will God do?

The Birth
of John Foretold

Luke 1

In the days of Herod, king of Judea,
there was a priest named Zechariah.
And he had a wife from the daughters
of Aaron. Her name was Elizabeth. They
were both righteous before God. They kept
all the commandments of the Lord. But they
had no child. For they were both old.

Now Zechariah was serving as priest
before God. He was chosen to enter
the temple of the Lord. There he burned
incense. A large group of people were
praying outside. And there appeared
to him an angel of the Lord. The angel
stood on the right side of the altar.
And Zechariah was afraid when he saw him.

But the angel said, "Do not be afraid.
Your prayer has been heard. Your wife
Elizabeth will have a son. You shall call his
name *John*. And you will have joy.
For he will be great before the Lord. He
will be filled with the Holy Spirit. And he
will turn many of the children of Israel
to the Lord their God."

incense

appeared

vision

signs

conceived

Ask

Who surprised Zechariah in the temple?

What good news did he tell Zechariah?

What happened to Zechariah?

Do

Try using your hands to talk. Give someone a message using signs.

How would you say, "I saw an angel"?

Pray

Heavenly Father, thank You for sending Your angel to Zechariah with good news. Help me believe the Good News that Jesus is my Savior. Amen.

Zechariah said, "How shall I know this? For I am an old man. My wife is old too."

And the angel said, "I am Gabriel. I stand in the presence of God. I bring you this good news. And behold, you will not be able to speak until the day that these things take place. For you did not believe my words."

The people were waiting for Zechariah. They were wondering at his delay in the temple. And when he came out, he was not able to speak to them. And they knew that he had seen a vision in the temple. And he kept making signs to them. For he could not talk.

And when his time of service was ended, he went home.

Soon Elizabeth conceived. She said, "The Lord has done this for me." ★

The Birth of Jesus Foretold

Luke 1

virgin

favored

conceive

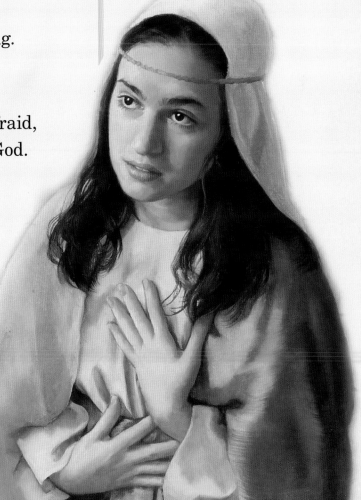

The angel Gabriel was sent from God to a city of Galilee. The city was named Nazareth. Gabriel came to a virgin. She was promised to marry a man whose name was Joseph. He was of the house of David. The virgin's name was Mary.

The angel said, "Greetings, O favored one. The Lord is with you!"

But Mary was troubled at the saying. She did not understand what sort of greeting this might be.

The angel said to her, "Do not be afraid, Mary. For you have found favor with God. Behold! You will conceive and have a Son. And you shall call His name *Jesus*. He will be great. He will be called the Son of the Most High. And the Lord God will give Him the throne. He will rule forever. His kingdom will never end."

Mary said to the angel, "How will this be, since I am a virgin?"

The angel said, "The Holy Spirit will come upon you. The power of the Most High will do this. So the child will be called holy—the Son of God.

"Behold! Your relative Elizabeth, who is old, is also going to have a baby. Nothing will be impossible with God."

Mary said, "Behold! I am the servant of the Lord. Let it be done according to your word."

Then the angel left. ✶

Ask

What did the angel say to Mary?

What did Mary say to the angel?

Do

Mary was the mother of Jesus. She lived in Nazareth.

What is your mother's name? Find out where she lived when you were born.

Pray

Heavenly Father, You chose Mary to be the mother of Jesus, my Savior. Thank You for choosing me to be Your child. Amen.

Mary Visits Elizabeth

fruit of your
womb

magnifies

Luke 1

The angel Gabriel told Mary, "Behold!
You will have a Son. You shall call His name
Jesus."

The angel also told her, "Your relative
Elizabeth, who is old, is also going to have
a baby."

In those days, Mary went quickly
to the hill country. She came to a town
in Judah. And she entered the house of
Zechariah. She greeted Elizabeth. And
Elizabeth heard Mary's greeting. Then the
baby leaped in Elizabeth's womb!

And Elizabeth was filled with the Holy
Spirit. She said with a loud cry, "Blessed
are you! And blessed is the fruit of your
womb. Behold! The sound of your greeting
came to my ears. Then the baby in my womb
leaped for joy."

And Mary said,

"My soul magnifies the Lord.

My spirit rejoices in God my Savior. For He
    has looked on me.

Behold! All people will call me blessed.

Ask

What did the baby inside Elizabeth do when he heard Mary's voice?

Was Mary happy to be the mother of Jesus?

Do

Mary said her soul magnified the Lord. She praised God with happy words.

You can magnify the Lord too. Use happy words to tell what God has done for you.

Pray

Heavenly Father, Mary praised You with happy words. I praise You too, for You have done great things for me. You sent Jesus to be my Savior. Amen.

The mighty God has done great things for me.

Holy is His name.

He gives mercy to those who trust in Him.

He has shown strength with His arm.

He has scattered the proud.

He has brought down the mighty.

He has lifted up the humble.

He has filled the hungry with good things.

He has sent away the rich with nothing.

He has helped His children."

Mary stayed with Elizabeth about three months. Then she went home. ★

The Birth of John

Luke 1

The time came. Elizabeth gave birth to a son. Her neighbors and relatives heard about the Lord's mercy to her. On the eighth day they came to rejoice.

They would have called the baby Zechariah. That was his father's name. But his mother said, "No. He shall be called *John*."

They said to her, "None of your relatives is called by this name." Then they made signs to Zechariah. He still could not speak. They asked him what he wanted the baby to be called.

Zechariah asked for a writing tablet. He wrote, "His name is John." And they all wondered.

Right away Zechariah spoke. He blessed God.

All these things were talked about through all the hill country. Everyone who heard them said, "What will this child be?"

Zechariah was filled with the Holy Spirit. He prophesied, saying,

mercy

prophesied

redeemed

prophets

salvation

Ask

When the baby was born, who came to rejoice with Zechariah and Elizabeth?

What did Zechariah and Elizabeth name the baby?

What did Zechariah say about the baby?

Do

God's people still sing Zechariah's happy words.

Make up a happy song about how God has blessed your family.

Pray

Heavenly Father, You sent John to tell people that Jesus was coming to forgive their sins. Thank You for grown-up people who tell me that Jesus loves me and can forgive the wrong things I think or say or do. Amen.

"Blessed be the Lord God.

He has visited His people.

He has redeemed His people.

He spoke by the mouth of His holy prophets.

He said we should be saved from our enemies.

Then we, being saved, might serve Him without fear.

And you, child, will be called the prophet of the Most High.

You will go before the Lord. You will prepare His ways.

You will make known salvation to His people.

You will tell about the forgiveness of sins.

For the tender mercy of our God will give light to those who sit in darkness.

God will guide our feet in the way of peace."

After this John grew. He became strong in spirit. And when he was older, he lived in the wilderness. ★

12

An Angel Visits Joseph

Matthew 1

Long, long ago, God told people about His promise to send a Savior. But before Jesus came to earth as a baby, God had to help people get ready.

Now the birth of Jesus Christ took place in this way. Mary and Joseph were planning to be married. They were betrothed. Before they came together, Mary was found to be with child from the Holy Spirit.

Joseph was a just man. He thought he would divorce Mary quietly. But as he thought about these things, an angel of the Lord came to him in a dream.

The angel said, "Joseph, son of David, do not be afraid. You can take Mary as your wife. The baby is from the Holy Spirit. She will have a Son. You shall call His name *Jesus*. He will save His people from their sins."

betrothed

divorce

prophet

Immanuel

commanded

Ask

What problem did Joseph have?

What did the angel tell Joseph?

What name would Joseph give the baby?

Do

Make an angel from an upside-down white paper cup. Use a marker to give the angel a face.

Have the angel repeat the words spoken to Joseph.

Pray

Dear God, I am so glad to know the truth that Jesus is my Immanuel. Amen.

Then Joseph knew Mary was telling the truth.

All this took place just as the Lord had spoken many years before. The prophet Isaiah said:

"Behold, the virgin shall conceive. She will have a Son. They shall call His name *Immanuel.*"

Immanuel means "God with us."

Joseph woke up from his sleep. He did what the angel of the Lord commanded him to do. He took Mary as his wife. Later, when the baby was born, Joseph called His name *Jesus.* ★

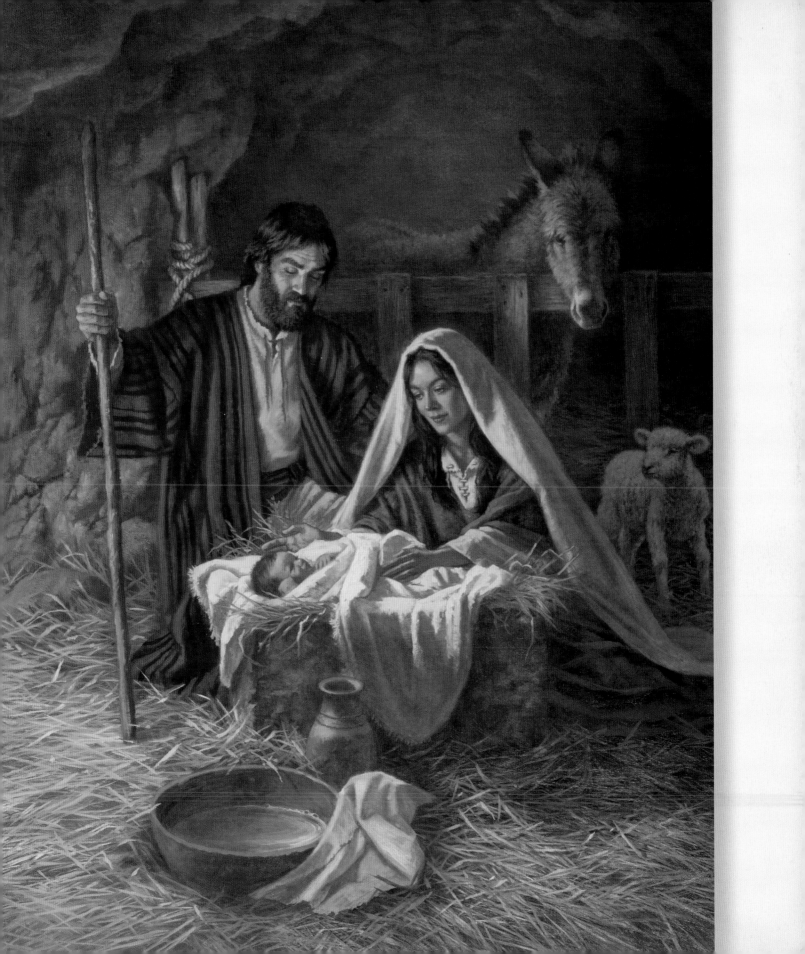

The Birth of Jesus

Luke 2

In those days the Roman ruler told all the people to register for a census. All went to be registered, each to his own town. Joseph also went to Bethlehem. He took Mary.

While they were there, the time came for her to give birth. She gave birth to her first child, a Son. She wrapped Him in cloths. She placed Him in a manger. For there was no room for them in the inn.

Not far away shepherds were in the field. They were watching their flock by night. An angel appeared. The glory of the Lord shone around them. They were filled with fear.

The angel said, "Fear not. For behold! I bring you good news of a great joy for all people. To you is born this day a Savior. He is Christ the Lord. You will find a baby wrapped in cloths and lying in a manger."

Suddenly there were many angels. They praised God and said,

"Glory to God in the highest,
and peace on earth!"

The angels went away. Then the shepherds said, "Let us go and see this thing."

register

census

manger

treasured

devout

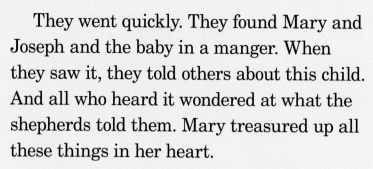

They went quickly. They found Mary and Joseph and the baby in a manger. When they saw it, they told others about this child. And all who heard it wondered at what the shepherds told them. Mary treasured up all these things in her heart.

At the end of eight days, the baby was called *Jesus*. This was the name given to Him by the angel before He was born.

When the time came, Joseph and Mary brought Jesus to the temple in Jerusalem.

A man in Jerusalem named Simeon was righteous and devout. The Holy Spirit revealed to him that he would not die before he had seen the Lord's Christ. Simeon was at the temple and took the baby in his arms. He blessed God and said,

"Lord, now let me go in peace.

My eyes have seen Your salvation.

He is a light to the Gentiles,
and a glory to Your people."

His father and mother wondered at what Simeon said about Jesus. Simeon blessed them.

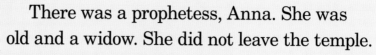

Ask

Where was Jesus born?

Who told the shepherds the good news about the baby?

Do

Use play dough and boxes to make a stable, manger, Mary, Joseph, and baby Jesus.

Pray

Dear Jesus,
I love to hear the story of Your birth. Glory to God! You came to be my Savior. Amen.

There was a prophetess, Anna. She was old and a widow. She did not leave the temple.

She worshiped God by fasting and praying night and day. She came and gave thanks to God. She spoke of Jesus to all.

When they had done all the Law said to do, Mary and Joseph went back to Nazareth. ✭

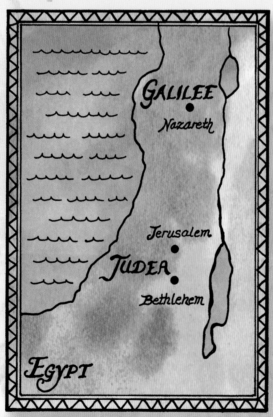

The Visit of the Wise Men

Matthew 2

After Jesus was born, Wise Men from the east came to Jerusalem. They asked King Herod, "Where is He who has been born King of the Jews? We saw His star and have come to worship Him."

When King Herod heard this, he was worried. He met with the chief priests and scribes. He asked them where the Christ was to be born.

They told him, "In Bethlehem. For that is written by the prophet."

Then Herod met secretly with the Wise Men. He asked them when the star had appeared. Then he sent them to Bethlehem. He said, "Go and search for the child. When you have found Him, tell me. I want to come and worship Him."

Jerusalem

chief priests

scribes

frankincense and myrrh

The Wise Men went on their way. Behold, the star went before them. It rested over the place where the child was. When they saw the star, they rejoiced.

They went into the house and saw the child with Mary, His mother. They knelt down and worshiped Jesus. Then they opened their treasures. They offered Him gifts of gold and frankincense and myrrh. And they were warned in a dream not to return to Herod. So they returned to their own country another way.

An angel of the Lord came to Joseph in a dream. The angel said, "Get up, and take the child and His mother. Flee to Egypt. Stay there until I tell you. For King Herod is about to search for the child, to destroy Him."

That night, Joseph took the child and His mother to Egypt. They stayed there until the death of King Herod. ★

Ask

What did God use to lead the Wise Men to Jesus?

How did God keep Jesus safe?

Do

Draw a Bible-times house and stars in the dark sky.

Draw one special star over the house.

Pray

Heavenly Father, thank You for leading the Wise Men to see and worship Jesus. Lead me to see Jesus and worship Him as my Savior. Amen.